The Yellowstone Park Fire of 1988

Melanie Ann Apel

rosen central™

The Rosen Publishing Group, Inc., New York

For Mom, Dad, Mindy, Michael, and Hayden

Published in 2004 by The Rosen Publishing Group, Inc.
29 East 21st Street, New York, NY 10010

First Edition

Library of Congress Cataloging-in-Publication Data
Apel, Melanie Ann.
The Yellowstone Park fire of 1988 / by Melanie Ann Apel. — 1st ed.
    p. cm. — (Tragic fires throughout history)
Summary: Describes the forest fire that burned one-third of Yellowstone National Park in the summer of 1988, including park history, causes of the fire, how the blaze was put out, and how the park recovered.
Includes bibliographical references and index.
ISBN 0-8239-4490-5 (library binding)
1. Forest fires—Yellowstone National Park—History—20th century—Juvenile literature. 2. Yellowstone National Park—History—20th century—Juvenile literature. 3. Fire ecology—Yellowstone National Park—Juvenile literature. [1. Forest fires—Yellowstone National Park. 2. Yellowstone National Park. 3. Fire ecology. 4. Ecology.]
I. Title. II. Series.
SD421.32.Y45A64 2004
634.9'618'0978752—dc21
                                                    2003010730

Manufactured in the United States of America

these amazing natural attractions are the park's geysers. Yellowstone National Park has more than 200 geysers, including one called Old Faithful and another called Steamboat. Old Faithful is famous for shooting up to 8,100 gallons (31.8 kiloliters) of hot water higher than 100 feet (30 meters) in the air approximately every seventy-eight minutes! Steamboat shoots up jets of water 195 to 375 feet (59 to 114 m) high. Geysers are caused by magma under the ground. The magma heats the water and causes all sorts of interesting sights!

Perhaps even more interesting, and maybe even more frightening, than the geysers of hot water is

This is a page from the 1872 act establishing Yellowstone as a national park. The national park system was created in 1864 by the state of California, which passed legislation to preserve the area now known as Yosemite National Park.

the volcano that used to erupt at the heart of Yellowstone. The last time the volcano erupted was about 600,000 years ago. The magma changed the face of the land of Yellowstone National Park. It pushed the ground upward, making it stretch and swell until it cracked open and all the ash and rock exploded from the crack in the earth. Today,

Old Faithful *(left)*, seen here sending water 150 feet (46 m) up into the air, is one of the best-known attractions in Yellowstone National Park. The Mammoth Hot Springs Terraces *(right)*, formed by calcium carbonate deposits, are also popular.

there is still a reserve of magma below the earth's surface in Yellowstone. This means that some day there may be another volcanic eruption in the park.

Lodgepole Pines

There are more lodgepole pines than any other type of tree in Yellowstone. In fact, 80 percent of the park's trees are lodgepole pines. While

CONTENTS

	Introduction	4
Chapter 1	Yellowstone National Park	6
Chapter 2	Fire!	12
Chapter 3	Putting Out the Blaze	26
Chapter 4	The Ashes Cool	32
	Timeline	41
	Glossary	43
	For More Information	44
	For Further Reading	45
	Bibliography	46
	Index	47

Introduction

Forest fires are not uncommon. While some forest fires can be rather small and nonthreatening, others can be devastating to the land and nearby communities. Forest fires start up with little or no warning and often burn for days, sometimes getting out of control. Eventually, either nature steps in to shower the fire with heavy rains, or firefighters are forced to try to get the blaze under control. When it's over, a forest fire can leave terrible destruction in its wake.

The environment itself changes every time a forest fire occurs. People living in most parts of the United States and Canada do not have to worry about forest fires simply because they do not live near a forest. But for the people who live in the western states and provinces, a forest fire is always a threat.

Yellowstone National Park has certainly seen its fair share of fires over the years. One year, however, the park experienced a series of fires that made the history books. That year was 1988, and the summer of fires is still remembered by people all over the United States.

Firefighters create a firebreak in Yellowstone on August 31, 1988. Firebreaks are long clearings that help stop wildfires from spreading.

Yellowstone National Park

Established in 1872, Yellowstone National Park attracts visitors from all over the world because of its breathtaking natural beauty and abundance of wildlife. And there's plenty to do, too! Visitors to the park can try kayaking, fishing, skiing, rafting, and snowmobiling. They can take a wildlife tour, celebrate at one of the park's many festivals throughout the year, or shop in a number of different art galleries.

Yellowstone National Park is located in the Rocky Mountains of the western United States. While most of the park's 2.2 million acres (890,312 hectares) lie in Wyoming, portions of the park spill into the neighboring states of Montana and Idaho.

Geysers and Other Natural Attractions

Yellowstone National Park is the largest, oldest, and most popular national park in the world. Much of its popularity is due to the fact that the park has some pretty interesting natural wonders. Among lodgepole pines grow at a fairly rapid rate, they do not live as long as other trees. The life span of a lodgepole pine is only about 200 years. Dying and dead lodgepole pines become weak and brittle and fall to the ground easily during stormy weather. The forest floor becomes a blanket of dead lodgepole pines, while at the same time young lodgepole pines are growing tall into the sky. Generally, all these dead lodgepole pines decay and eventually disappear, becoming one with the earth again. But this can happen only if they get very wet from a great deal of rain. Rainwater soaks the dead lodgepole pines through,

allowing bacteria and fungus to move in and break down the wood. Yellowstone sees little of this because it tends to be dry compared to other forests in the region. Therefore, the lodgepole pines simply remain where they fall, making it nearly impossible for people to walk through. Additionally, the buildup of fallen trees can set the scene for quick-catching, fast-moving fires.

These bison attempt to graze in the ruins of the lodgepole pine forest that was once their home. This section of the forest was destroyed during the 1988 fires.

Rules for Fires

Wild forest fires have burned in Yellowstone for hundreds of

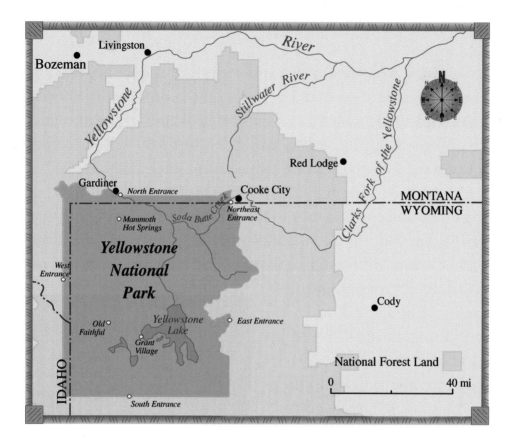

This map details the boundaries of Yellowstone's 2.2 million acres (890,000 hectares), most of which fall within Wyoming. It is the largest park in the United States.

years. The way they have been handled, however, has been an ever-changing story. Back in the 1700s and even before, wildfires simply burned uncontrolled. There was not much people could do about them besides getting out of the way. However, once more people began to settle in the area and make their homes on the land, there was some need for a change in the way fires were handled. Once the land was designated a national park in 1872, things had to change as well. At that time, it was believed that all fires were bad—no matter how large or small. People who lived on and cared for the land thought that fires should be put out as soon as possible before they could do much damage. This way of thinking continued through the first part of the twentieth century.

These trucks are carrying members of the Civilian Conservation Corps. They are on their way to contain a fire in the Kaniksu National Forest in Idaho in 1934.

In the 1940s, studies done by ecologists began to change peoples' thinking regarding what should be done about forest fires. The ecologists came to the conclusion that fire was a necessary part of nature and that the changes fire brought to the land were, in fact, good. As a result, in the 1950s and 1960s, national parks and forests started experimenting to see what would happen if they controlled the fires but did not actually put them out. The results were favorable, and in the 1970s, Yellowstone National Park began a new natural fire management plan, which let any fire that was started by a lightning strike burn itself out.

Fire!

The summer of 1988 began like it always had in the Rocky Mountain states. But as June turned into July, it became obvious this would be a summer unlike any other. The events that would soon take place in Yellowstone National Park would make history.

That summer was marked by an unusual series of forest fires—huge forest fires that even teams of firefighters numbering in the thousands could not put out. Yellowstone had not seen such terrible forest fires in more than 200 years.

Two Hundred Years in the Making

Forest fires occur in nature as a way of keeping things in balance. If there are no fires, things may grow wildly unchecked. This is what had been happening in Yellowstone until the summer of 1988.

For more than 200 years, trees and forests grew abundantly in Yellowstone. Although there was a fair share of good-sized forest fires in the 1800s, really grand fires had not burned in Yellowstone since the early 1700s. Approaching 300 years without a major fire, there was a great deal of dead wood lying about the forest floor. Like a campfire or a well-stocked fireplace, Yellowstone National Park was ready to burn. Nevertheless, the forest fires of the summer of 1988 came as quite a surprise.

A Hot, Dry Summer

Yellowstone was used to long, cold winters and short summers with a decent amount of rain. It was assumed that the summer of 1988 would be an especially rainy summer, just as the previous summers of the 1980s had been. Although the last six winters had seen little snowfall and things grew drier and drier, many people still believed Yellowstone could never fall victim to any serious forest fires.

There was a great deal of rain in the spring of 1988, more than usual for that time of year. By surprising contrast, the expected rain for the summer did not come. The sun blazed upon Yellowstone in the summer of 1988. Only 20 percent of the average June rainfall came. July was even worse, with practically no rain at all in the first weeks of the month. It was so hot and dry that water levels in the park's rivers and lakes began to drop, while smaller bodies of water such as streams and ponds dried up completely. The earth itself cracked in many places, allowing the sun to reach the underground water supplies. These dried up as well. It was Yellowstone's driest summer on record since 1872, the year the park was established.

Although storms loomed above, complete with cracking lightning and loud thunder, there continued to be little rain. The forests grew

Lightning is responsible for the majority of the forest fires Yellowstone experiences every year.

terribly dry. Lightning striking dried-out trees started to spark forest fires. The first of these fires occurred on May 24. This fire was, luckily, rather small and did little damage before rainfall later that same day put it out. Twenty fires started early in the season, and of those, eleven went out naturally. The others were being watched carefully by park officials according to the fire management plan. Although not an unusual fire itself, the fire of May 24 would mark the beginning of a terrible season for Yellowstone National Park.

Lightning Strikes

Lightning strikes started fires all over the park. Allowed to burn, most of the fires put themselves out. By mid-July 1988, there was still little rainfall in Yellowstone, and the forests remained dry. Fires were already swallowing many acres of the forest. A fire in the southern part of Yellowstone near Shoshone Lake was caused by lightning that struck on June 23. Two days later, lightning ignited another fire in the northwest part of the park. Although there was not enough rain to put these fires out, firefighters left the fires to burn.

These forest fires were fierce in the dry heat. They moved quickly and with great noise. Smoke from these fires was reported to have traveled as far east as Minneapolis, Minnesota, and as far west as the state of Washington. The smell of the smoke was so strong that people traveling by airplane far above the forest reported smelling it while aboard their planes.

Let the Fire Burn

Since 1972, the official policy on fires in Yellowstone was to let wildfires burn themselves out. Scientists had discovered that this was the best thing for the forest, as they studied nature and came to understand that fire had a special role in nature and a reason for existing. What they learned was that without fire, the dry forests were storing important nutrients in their trees—both the living ones and the dead ones. Without these nutrients, new trees had a hard time growing, and existing trees were suffering as well. They also discovered that fires help keep the smaller trees from invading the wide open spaces of land, where animals such as elk and buffalo like to graze. Without such fires, the grazing land would become overrun with trees, and certain animals would die out from lack of food.

Because of the way nature works, firefighters in Yellowstone National Park had been instructed to step in only if people's lives or property were in immediate danger. Fires were carefully monitored to be sure they were not burning out of control, threatening lives, becoming too dangerous, or causing any serious damage to the timber industry.

The policy regarding fires at Yellowstone National Park had been effective for fifteen years. According to the Web site Yellowstone Park Net, 233 fires had been left to burn in the park without incident during those fifteen years. In fact, the majority of these, a full 205, burned less than one acre each before they burned themselves out. Of

A car makes its way through the park in September 1988. The fires in the park sent smoke more than 20,000 feet (6,100 m) into the air.

the other twenty-eight fires that burned in the fifteen-year time span, the largest burned an area equal to just 1/300th of the park's land, or about 7,396 acres (2,993 ha). People in and around Yellowstone National Park were happy that the policy seemed to be working.

A Change in Policy

By the middle of July 1988, 8,500 acres (3,440 ha) of Yellowstone National Park's land had burned. By July 31, 115,000 acres (46,538 ha) had burned. At this point, enough damage had been done that park officials had grown concerned. It was clear that the park's policy regarding the handling of fires had to be changed. On July 21, officials declared that firefighters were to tackle and extinguish every fire that blazed in Yellowstone. The very next day, firefighters put out a small fire in the Targhee National Forest, which is located just west of Yellowstone National Park.

Firefighters

As soon as the official firefighting policy was changed, fire-fighters began to battle the flames of two fires that had already been burning since the second week in July. By this time, the two fires had met and joined together. Now one large fire, it earned a name: the Clover-Mist Fire. Hundreds of firefighters worked around the clock to extinguish the many blazes that attacked Yellowstone National Park that summer. They fought

These firefighters use Pulaskis, special firefighting tools with an ax on one end and a hoe on the other, to create a firebreak. Other firefighters use hoses to wet the underbrush.

the fires from the ground and from above, using helicopters and airplanes. But it was no use. Lightning continued to strike, and fires ignited all over the park.

Nearby national forests were suffering from their own fires as well. Some of these fires caught the wind and made their way to Yellowstone, adding to the park's existing blazes. Firefighters worked to the point of exhaustion, but without the help of much needed rain, they were making little progress controlling the fires.

Fanning the Flames

To make matters worse, winds began to kick in. Just two days following the policy change, the winds became as fierce as the fires themselves. Cold fronts were passing through the area, bringing with them winds so strong they might as well have been hurricanes. Gusts blowing 60 to 80 miles per hour (96 to 128 km/h) whipped through Yellowstone and carried the fire along. While it might seem as if a strong gust of wind might

When forest fires become too large for firefighters to extinguish from the ground, planes are called in to fight the blaze from the air.

work well to blow out a fire, like blowing out birthday candles, the opposite is true. Rather than blowing the fire out, the winds carried oxygen to the fires. Fire needs oxygen to continue burning. The winds acted as a feeding source to keep the fires alive. The winds also helped bring smaller fires together, creating larger fires everywhere.

The scene was horrible. Tops of trees charred. Boulders exploded from the intensity of the heat. Clouds of smoke blocked out the sun for days on end.

Nothing got in the way of the wall of flames that raced through Yellowstone. Neither rivers, canyons, parking lots, nor roads stopped the flames. The flames moved an average of five miles (8 km) every day. One larger fire, however, moved 14 miles (23 km) in just four hours! Giant embers as large as a clenched fist exploded from the flames, sometimes traveling as far as a mile (1.6 km) and igniting new fires where they landed.

North Fork Fire

One of the larger fires to burn in Yellowstone that summer would become known as the North Fork Fire. In its first day, the North Fork Fire grew to cover 500 acres (202 ha). The dryness of the trees and the fierceness of the wind was a terrible combination. Despite the firefighters' best efforts, there was little they could accomplish. On July 22, the North Fork Fire had begun in the nearby Targhee National Forest when a firefighter carelessly tossed a cigarette to the ground without extinguishing it. By July 23, the fire had burned 1,300 acres (526 ha). Even the efforts of parachuting firefighters, called smokejumpers, were fruitless.

The Old Faithful Inn Is Threatened

The North Fork Fire caught the wind and took a twisting path into Yellowstone, then back to the Targhee National Forest. It moved frighteningly close to the town of West Yellowstone before turning back into the park itself. Unheeded by rivers or roads, the blaze moved toward Old Faithful and the Old Faithful

The Old Faithful Inn, built from lodgepole pine logs, was nearly consumed by the fires as they raged out of control. If the direction of the wind hadn't changed at the last minute, the inn would have burned down.

Inn. The historic inn is the largest building in the world built entirely of logs.

Even before the fire itself could be seen, the roar of the fire could be heard, and black smoke made its way into the area. Firefighters in the air dropped water and special chemicals to try to put out the fire before it reached the inn. Exhausted firefighters on the ground wet down buildings in the area. It seemed, however, no matter how hard they tried, nothing would stop the blaze and the inn would surely be destroyed. Only a

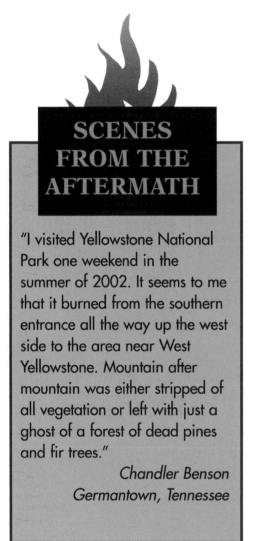

miracle could save the Old Faithful Inn. And that's exactly what happened. Just in the nick of time, the wind shifted. The fire turned toward the northeast, and the Old Faithful Inn escaped any serious harm. Thankfully, the Old Faithful Inn had recently been equipped with a new sprinkler system on its roof. This helped the desperate situation as well. Despite the Old Faithful Inn's good fortune, however, about twenty small buildings nearby met a much worse fate.

August Arrives, Little Changes

By the end of July, the fires of Yellowstone National Park were uncontrollable. Fire experts from all over the United States were being called in. Together at Yellowstone they talked in earnest about what was happening and what could be done to control the fires. After much discussion, they agreed that no matter what was in store, they doubted that the fires would burn much more than about 200,000 acres (80,937 ha) of Yellowstone National Park.

Unfortunately, the fire experts' predictions were wrong. Before the middle of August had settled in, 201,000 acres (81,342 ha) of Yellowstone had already been consumed by flames, according to Idahonews.com. Fires threatened more and more of the forests of Yellowstone every day. People living nearby began to fear for their homes. Communities in and around the park were in danger of being consumed by the North Fork Fire. Canyon Village had to be evacuated on August 24, when the fire was just 5 miles (8 km) away from the village. At least 500 people, mostly employees of the park and tourists, were evacuated. Silver Gate and Cooke City, Montana, which both sit near the northeast corner of Yellowstone National Park, were soon threatened. The residents of these communities were very fortunate that firefighters were able to control the blaze and keep their communities from harm. But there was still more to come.

Black Saturday

Despite the summer's bad start, nothing could prepare Yellowstone for the fire that blazed on August 20. On the day that came to be remembered as Black Saturday, 165,000 acres (66,773 ha) in Yellowstone National Park and nearby forests burned, according to Yellowstone Park Net. Eighty-mile-per-hour (129 km/h) winds

Slurry, a chemical mixture used as a flame retardant, is sprayed on buildings in danger of being consumed by the fire.

whipped through Yellowstone with the force of a hurricane. Every fire that was already burning caught the gust and grew even larger.

The North Fork Fire was blown to an area where, over the years, strong winds had knocked down a large number of trees. Once again, this area could be compared to a well-logged fireplace, prime to blaze.

Another fire, named the Hellroaring Fire, was only five days old on August 20. Although it had started just north of Yellowstone National Park, it soon consumed 30,000 acres (12,141 ha) of the park.

It had just about died out by this point, but the Storm Creek Fire also caught the wind. Brought back to life, this fire covered more than 10 miles (16 km) of land in just three hours.

Although 2,000 firefighters fought the blaze, they were truly helpless against its force. Instead, they took care of the park buildings and kept them from catching fire. Once again, the historic Old Faithful Inn was threatened. Eight major fires were burning by the beginning of September, and one of these, the raging North Fork, crept toward the historic log cabin.

September 10

Although summer would officially be over in less than two weeks, the fires of the summer of 1988 were still burning at full force on September 10. By this day, the park headquarters, located at Mammoth Hot Springs, was in danger of destruction by flames from the North Fork Fire. Tower Junction, a breathtaking landscape of pine-covered canyons, stood just a quarter of a mile from another arm of the North Fork Fire. To make matters worse, the day's forecast called for winds gusting up to 60 miles per hour (97 km/h).

By the early afternoon, however, things began to look better. The sky had opened, and it was raining all around Old Faithful. By the morning of September 11, snow had begun to fall and was now covering the streets of West Yellowstone. Nature had, as was expected, finally stepped in and taken care of itself. The end of the fires was in sight. Although small fires continued to burn into November, the fiery summer of 1988 had at last come to an end.

Putting Out the Blaze

Firefighters had used many different types of tools as well as various strategies to try to put out the fires. Working from the sky above, helicopters had scooped water from nearby rivers and lakes and dropped the water onto the flames. Larger airplanes had dropped special fire-retardant chemicals onto the flames. Down on the ground, firefighters had used Pulaskis to cut down trees and dig up the ground in hopes that the broken-up surface would slow the fires. Bulldozers, which were not usually allowed inside Yellowstone because of the damage they do to the ground, had been allowed in. The firefighters hoped that the bulldozers' tracks would break up the ground and thereby halt the path of the fires.

None of these efforts worked. It had soon become apparent that no human effort would be enough to fight the tremendous fires raging through Yellowstone National Park in the summer of 1988.

Why Couldn't They Stop It?

Many of Yellowstone's trees were in various stages of decay, and many more were dead, having fallen victim to bark beetles. Some

of the dead trees remained
standing while others lay strewn
about the forest floor. Still other
trees were simply dried out. All
of these trees made excellent
fuel for the flames as they
approached each new area.
Some kinds of fires are more
difficult to fight than others.
Canopy fires are those that
start at the tops of the trees.
Burning from the top branches
down, these fires are extremely
hot. They also move rapidly
from treetop to treetop. Canopy
fires can be especially hard to

Firefighters attempt to put out the blazes from the air, but their efforts make little difference.

stop. Crowning also took a great number of trees completely
down. Crowning occurs when the tops of the trees, called the
crowns, catch fire, and before much time has passed, entire trees
have been engulfed in flames.

One serious danger to the firefighters themselves was
firebrands. Firebrands are like great walls of fire. They move
quickly, especially when they have a good wind behind them.
Moving from one area to another, they start more and more
fires as they go. The danger to firefighters comes when the
firebrands whip up quickly and move in behind the area
where the firefighters are working on another fire. With little

Fifty-five-mile-per-hour (88.5 km/h) winds drive fires in the North Fork section of the park across the highway. Some of the fires were so large that neither roadways nor waterways were able to halt their progress.

notice, the firefighters are soon surrounded by fire and can become trapped!

Animal Casualties

Although there was no way to accurately count the total number of animals that might have lost their lives in the Yellowstone National Park fires of 1988, estimates were made and the results were far from devastating, all things considered. Counting the bodies of small animals found after the fires was all but impossible. Counting the larger animals was not such a laborious task. No more than about 400 large animals were found dead after the fires burned out. According to Yellowstone Park Net, most of the dead animals were elk, about 345 of the 40,000 to 50,000 that roam freely in the area. The rest of the death toll was small: approximately thirty-six deer, twelve moose, six black bears, and nine bison died in the greater Yellowstone area. Two radio-collared grizzly bears were missing immediately after the fires. It was assumed that both were dead, but several years later one returned.

Most of the animals died because the fire trapped them and there was no safe direction in which to escape. A few fish died as well. Although it is not known for certain how they died, it is believed that the fish died either from poisoning by the fire-retardant chemicals or because the water they were swimming in became too hot for them to survive.

Thousands of animals roam freely in Yellowstone, and the relatively low number of dead animals can be credited to the natural instincts of the animals themselves. When they realized fire was coming, they simply got out of the way! Many elk, bison, pronghorn, and deer saved their own lives in this manner. Even more animals watched from nearby, grazing as they kept their eyes on the blaze.

Birds hunted for food during the fire and did well for themselves. Small animals, in their attempts to escape, became quick meals for larger birds. While many birds took flight and escaped the fire

When the fires did finally cool and burn out completely in November 1988, the statistics were staggering.

- Of the 2.2 million acres (890,308 ha) that make up Yellowstone National Park, 793,880 acres (321,272 ha) had been burned to some extent, according to the Web site of the National Park Service.

- Thirty-eight percent of the fires were ground, or surface, fires. Fifty-seven percent of the fires had been canopy fires. The other 5 percent of the fires had burned over meadows and grasslands.

- In the entire Greater Yellowstone area, a total of 1.2 million acres (485,623 ha) had been touched by fire, according to the National Park Service.

- Yellowstone Park Net notes that more than $120 million had been spent in efforts to put out the many fires that blazed through Yellowstone in the summer of 1988. In all, more than 25,000 firefighters had taken part in fighting the fires. At times, it was estimated that 9,000 firefighters had been working all at the same time.

In time, the charred forest that this elk calf walks through will regrow, as will the calf's singed coat.

easily, many others met a different fate. As they had escaped from the blaze itself, many birds died on the roads outside the burning area. Because the dense smoke made it hard for firefighters and birds alike to see, it was not uncommon for cars and trucks on the road to hit and kill unsuspecting birds. Along the roads, owls, hawks, flickers, grouse, and other birds were found dead.

The Ashes Cool

Between May and September 1988, eight separate and very large fires had broken out in Yellowstone National Park, raging wildly and causing unthinkable and unstoppable destruction. Many other smaller fires added to the devastation as well. In fact, in the area considered Greater Yellowstone, there were as many as 248 fires in the summer of 1988. Only fifty of these smaller fires had taken place in Yellowstone National Park itself. Once the policy on fighting fires was changed in the middle of July, many of the fires were battled by firefighters and volunteers. Three of the fires that firefighters had tried to control right from the start had been started by careless humans. Only thirty-one fires had been allowed to burn. Of these fires, twenty-eight had started within Yellowstone National Park itself.

Believe it or not, no one died in Yellowstone directly because of the fires of 1988. The only two deaths during the blazing summer occurred outside the park. One firefighter died when he was hit by a falling tree. Another firefighter died in a plane crash while transporting other people to help fight the fires.

In the Media

Television news and newspaper headlines across the United States told of the destruction that had occurred in Yellowstone. Many of the stories said that there was nothing left of the park. Reading and hearing the news made it easy to believe that the entire area of Yellowstone National Park had been ravaged beyond recognition and that there was nothing left of the land that had once been a beautiful national treasure.

Colorado's KCNC-TV news team sets up its equipment near the scene of the fires. Many news reporters overestimated the extent of the fire damage while underestimating the resiliency of the park.

Luckily, the opposite was true. Plenty of what makes Yellowstone National Park so special survived the summer of fires. In fact, even with such furious flames, the fires touched only one-third of the park. None of the fragile hot springs, geysers, or steam vents had been damaged. The various park communities had also escaped harm.

SCENES FROM THE AFTERMATH

"In 1972 my husband and I hiked into Grebe Lake in Yellowstone Park to do some camping. It was an easy three-mile [4.8-km] hike through lush vegetation. Twenty years later, in 1992, we hiked through the same area with our two sons, but the scenery was completely different. Although the great Yellowstone fire had swept through this area five years earlier, the forest was still a blackened ruin—at least at first glance. Upon further investigation, we discovered small plants pushing their way through the charred remains. It was a life-affirming sight. I hope to return to Yellowstone in 2012 to see the forest's progress in its recovery from the fire."

Laurie Swindler
Normal, Illinois

Healing, as Usual

One might also think that once a fire—or fires—of such magnitude has swept through a park and caused such damage, nothing would or could ever be the same again. In a large sense, this is very true. Nothing in Yellowstone National Park would be the same again. But this was okay. Nature would take care of Yellowstone and help it grow anew.

As you read at the beginning of this book, forest fires are not uncommon. Because of this, nature has a way of taking care of itself, of rebuilding after such fires. In fact, fire has been such a regular part of Yellowstone that much of the way it looks today is owed to nature renewing and reshaping the landscape after such fires. Fire is a natural occurrence and, in fact, a necessary one to keep things in balance. It takes a long time for a forest or park to heal after a fire or fires, such as those that blazed through Yellowstone in the summer of 1988. But the park will heal. Nature will make sure of that.

The Lodgepole Pines Reseed

The lodgepole pines worked hard to help their forest rebuild itself after the fires of 1988. Logdepole pines have two types of cones: one type can open by itself, the other type cannot. This second type of lodgepole pinecone is sealed shut with a sticky resin. Luckily, the seeds inside the resin-sealed cones are made to live for many years. In fact, they actually lie waiting inside the cone to be released by none

Plants on the forest floor often thrive after dense forest canopy is burned away. These low-lying plants will receive more sunlight, allowing them to flourish.

other than a fire! It takes temperatures rising to hotter than 113°F (45°C) for the resin to finally melt. Once the resin melts away, the cones can open up and release the seeds, which are then scattered about the floor of the forest. Once reseeded, the forest will begin anew. Therefore, fire can be seen as not only good but necessary in this case.

Thriving in Spite of— Because of—Fire

Fireweed is a lovely pink flower that is tall and cone shaped. But fireweed grows well only if it can see the sun, which it cannot if tall trees cast shade over it. When fires, such as those that burned in 1988, destroy the tall trees, the fireweed has a chance to blossom. A strong plant, this flower's stem is protected underground from the heat of the fire. With seeds similar to that of a dandelion, the wind often carries the fireweed seeds off to the burned areas of the forest. There, the fireweed takes root in the earth, and in a year, a bright pink floor dazzles among the charred remains of the previous year's fire.

Researchers checked the soil in the badly burned areas of Yellowstone. To their delight, the roots of plants and bushes, as well as their seeds, were still alive underground. There would be regrowth for certain.

A New Face

Yellowstone National Park looks different today than it looked before the fires of 1988. This is the way nature works, and the new face now worn by Yellowstone is a welcomed one. The reason this works well for the animals who live in Yellowstone is because now there is a larger variety of home environments for the animals. New plants will thrive in their newfound sunlight, and larger animals will be able to move more quickly through the now-cleared pathways.

It took less than a year for Yellowstone to begin to regrow

SCENES FROM THE AFTERMATH

"I remember the Yellowstone fire well. I remember thinking, 'I've been there.' I was there in the summer of 1983, when I was eleven. Later, in 1995, my husband and I drove through the area again, and even after more than seven years we could still see the destruction. Oh, things had grown back, there were little trees. But there were tall trees that still bore the burn marks from the fire. They don't just go in and clean up after a fire since the area is a preserve. They just let nature take its course."

Jennifer Logothetti Gordon
Glenview, Illinois

and heal itself following the devastating fires of 1988. New flowers and different types of grasses were already growing and blossoming the next spring. In fact, the nitrogen and various other nutrients that were released during the fires even helped the new growth, nourishing plants and grassy meadows to grow more lustrously than before. Even the animals that graze on the grass were getting an improved diet. Because some plants and animals prefer the recently burned areas, whereas others prefer the areas that have not burned, the populations shifted within Yellowstone after the fires. Once again, nature proves that the fires were necessary and efficient for Yellowstone and its inhabitants.

The following spring did not see the decline in visitors that park officials feared. Less than a year after the fires, visitors to Yellowstone were as abundant as ever.

About ten years after the fires, Yellowstone had seen almost a complete recovery. The new trees were tall enough to be considered a young forest. The floor of the forest was covered with a healthy green carpet. Dead trees had shed their bark and now stood tall and silvery in the sunlight.

Revising the Policy Again

Because of the fires in Yellowstone and the fact that the fire management policy had to be changed in the middle of the disaster that was occurring that summer, all parks in the United

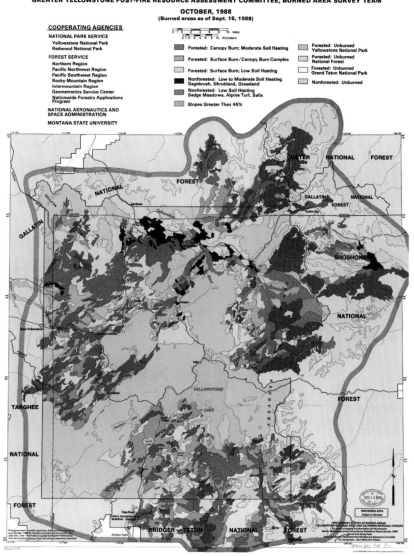

PRELIMINARY SURVEY OF BURNED AREAS:
YELLOWSTONE NATIONAL PARK AND ADJOINING NATIONAL FORESTS
GREATER YELLOWSTONE POST-FIRE RESOURCE ASSESSMENT COMMITTEE, BURNED AREA SURVEY TEAM

OCTOBER, 1988
(Burned areas as of Sept. 15, 1988)

COOPERATING AGENCIES

NATIONAL PARK SERVICE
Yellowstone National Park
Redwood National Park

FOREST SERVICE
Northern Region
Pacific Northwest Region
Pacific Southwest Region
Rocky Mountain Region
Intermountain Region
Geometronics Service Center
Nationwide Forestry Applications Program

NATIONAL AERONAUTICS AND SPACE ADMINISTRATION

MONTANA STATE UNIVERSITY

Forested: Canopy Burn; Moderate Soil Heating
Forested: Surface Burn/Canopy Burn Complex
Forested: Surface Burn; Low Soil Heating
Nonforested: Low to Moderate Soil Heating Sagebrush, Shrubland, Grassland
Nonforested: Low Soil Heating Sedge Meadows, Alpine Turf, Salix
Slopes Greater Than 45%

Forested: Unburned Yellowstone National Park
Forested: Unburned National Forest
Forested: Unburned Grand Teton National Park
Nonforested: Unburned

This map details the areas of the park that suffered fire damage. Understanding the way the fires spread will help firefighters devise more effective fire management plans. The orange, red, and burgundy sections depict fire damage of low, moderate, and high.

A young lodgepole pine seedling pushes its way up through the charred remains of older trees in Yellowstone.

States were forced to take a look at their own fire management plans. A panel of independent scientists helped the country's national parks create an updated plan after assessing the damage from an ecological standpoint. By 1992, Yellowstone National Park had a new wildland fire management plan. This plan calls for stricter guidelines under which fires that occur naturally are allowed to burn.

What Happens Next?

Nature has a way of making certain that whatever needs to happen will happen. This is why you can be sure that there will be some large forest fires in Yellowstone National Park again. These fires may come far in the future. But rest assured that sometime around 2088 or 2138—approximately 100 to 150 years after the fires of 1988—the trees that are now still so young will begin to weaken and die off. As they fall to the forest floor, they set the stage for another round of fires, sometime in the 2400s, and yet another new beginning for the forest.

Timeline

Early 1700s
The last really grand fires burn on the land later known as Yellowstone National Park.

1800s
The area that would come to be known as Yellowstone National Park sees a number of good-sized forest fires.

1872
Yellowstone National Park is officially designated.

1940s
Ecologists realize that fire is a necessary part of nature and that the changes fire brings to the land are actually good. These discoveries change the thinking regarding what should be done about forest fires.

1950s and 1960s
National parks and forests experiment to see what happens if they control fires but do not actually put them out.

1972
Official policy on fires at Yellowstone is changed to allow wildfires started by lightning strikes to burn themselves out.

May 24, 1988
The terrible fire season of 1988 officially starts with a lightning strike that causes a small fire that does little damage. Rainfall later that day puts it out.

June 23, 1988
A lightning strike starts a fire in the southern part of Yellowstone near Shoshone Lake.

June 25, 1988

Lightning starts another fire in the northwest part of the park. There is not enough rain to put this fire out, and firefighters let it burn.

July 21, 1988

Park officials declare that firefighters are to tackle and extinguish every fire that blazes in Yellowstone.

July 22, 1988

The North Fork Fire begins to burn.

July 23, 1988

The North Fork Fire has already consumed 1,300 acres (526 ha), despite firefighters' attempts to extinguish it.

Late July, 1988

Two fires burning since the second week in July join together, creating one large fire called the Clover-Mist Fire.

Mid-August, 1988

More than 200,000 acres (80,937 ha) of Yellowstone have been consumed by flames.

August 20, 1988

Black Saturday. More than 165,000 acres (66,773 ha) burn in Yellowstone National Park and nearby forests.

September 11, 1988

Snow begins to fall. The end of the fires is in sight.

November, 1988

The last of the remaining small fires burn themselves out.

1992

Yellowstone National Park declares a new, updated fire management plan calling for stricter guidelines under which fires that occur naturally are allowed to burn.

1998

Yellowstone sees almost complete recovery.

Glossary

bacteria (bak-TEER-ee-uh) Any of numerous microscopic organisms that are single-celled and important to nature because of their chemical activities and as causes of diseases.

ember (EM-bur) A glowing piece of coal or wood in the ashes of a fire.

extinguish (ex-TING-wish) To cause to stop burning.

flicker (FLIK-er) A large North American bird, similar to a woodpecker.

fungus (FUN-gis) Any of a large group of plants (as mushrooms, molds, and rusts) that have no chlorophyll and must live on other plants or animals or on decaying material.

geyser (GY-zer) A spring that now and then shoots up hot water and steam.

grouse (GRAUS) A game bird that is much like a domestic fowl.

magma (MAG-muh) Molten rock within the earth.

molten (MOHL-tun) Melted, especially by very great heat.

nutrients (NOO-tree-ints) Substances used in nutrition.

pronghorn (PRONG-horn) An animal similar to an antelope that lives in the treeless parts of the western United States and Mexico.

resin (REH-zin) A yellowish or brownish substance obtained from the gum or sap of some trees (as the pine) and used in varnish and medicine.

retardant (rih-TAR-dunt) Chemical used to slow, keep back, or delay a fire.

For More Information

National Wildfire Coordinating Group
National Interagency Fire Center
3833 South Development Avenue
Boise, ID 83705
Web site: http://www.nwcg.gov

USDA Forest Service
United States Department of Agriculture
P.O. Box 96090
Washington, DC 20090-6090
(202) 205-1661
(202) 205-1765
Web site: http://www.fs.fed.us/global

Web Sites

Due to the changing nature of Internet links, the Rosen Publishing Group, Inc., has developed an online list of Web sites related to the subject of this book. This site is updated regularly. Please use this link to access the list:

http://www.rosenlinks.com/tfth/ypfn

For Further Reading

Cottrell, William H. *Born of Fire: The Volcanic Origin of Yellowstone National Park*. Boulder, CO: Roberts Rinehart Pub., 1987.

Lauber, Patricia. *Yellowstone 1988: Summer of Fire*. New York: Orchard Books, 1991.

Meister, Cari. *Yellowstone National Park* (Going Places). Edina, MN: Checkerboard Library, 2001.

Patent, Dorothy Hinshaw. *Yellowstone Fires: Flames and Rebirth*. New York: Holiday House, 1990.

Petersen, David. *Yellowstone National Parks* (True Books: National Parks). Danbury, CT: Children's Press, 2001.

Vogel, Carole Garnbuny, and Kathryn Allen Goldner. *The Great Yellowstone Fire*. San Francisco: Sierra Club Books, 1990.

Vogt, Gregory. *Forests on Fire: The Fight to Save Our Trees*. New York: Franklin Watts, 1990.

Bibliography

Benson, Chandler. E-mail interview by author, February 2003.

Davis, Kenneth C. *Don't Know Much About the 50 States*. New York: HarperCollins, 2001.

Gordon, Jennifer Logothetti. Telephone interview by author, Glenview, IL, December 2002.

Lauber, Patricia. *Yellowstone 1988: Summer of Fire*. New York: Orchard Books, 1991.

Patent, Dorothy Hinshaw. *Yellowstone Fires: Flames and Rebirth*. New York: Holiday House, 1990.

Scholastic Reference Staff. *Scholastic Atlas of the World*. New York: Scholastic, 2001.

Swindler, Laurie. E-mail interview by author, February 2003.

Index

A
animals, 15, 28–29, 31, 37, 38

B
Black Saturday, 23–24

C
Clover-Mist Fire, 17
communities, 10, 16, 23

F
firebrands, 27–28
firefighters, 4, 12, 15, 17–18, 20, 21,
    23, 24, 26, 27–28, 30, 31, 32
fire management plan, 11, 14, 15, 16,
    17, 19, 32, 38, 40
fires
    and balance in nature, 12, 35, 38
    controlling, 11, 17–18, 22, 23, 26
    letting them burn out, 14, 15, 16,
      30, 32, 40
    small, 4, 14, 19, 25, 32
    started by people, 9, 20, 32
    types, 27, 30
    uncontrolled, 10, 12, 16, 19–20, 22,
      24, 32
fireweed, 36

G
geysers, 7, 34

H
Hellroaring Fire, 24

L
lightning, 11, 13, 14–15, 18
lodgepole pines, 8–9, 35–36

N
North Fork Fire, 20, 23, 24, 25

O
Old Faithful, 7, 20, 25
Old Faithful Inn, 20–21, 22, 24, 25

R
rain, 4, 9, 13, 14, 15, 18, 25
Rocky Mountains, 6, 12

S
smoke, 15, 19, 21
Storm Creek Fire, 24

T
Targhee National Forest, 17, 20
trees, 8–9, 12, 13, 14, 15, 19, 24, 26,
    27, 36, 38

W
West Yellowstone, 20, 25
wind, 18, 19, 20, 22, 23, 24, 25

Y

Yellowstone National Park, 4, 6–9, 11, 12–13, 17, 33, 34, 37, 38, 40

acreage burned in 1988, 14, 17, 20, 23, 30

fires in summer 1998, 4, 13–25, 26–31, 32, 33, 34, 35, 37, 38, 40

historic fires in, 9–11, 12–13

About the Author

Melanie Ann Apel has written more than forty nonfiction books for children and young adults. She holds a bachelor's degree in theater arts from Bradley University and another from National Lewis University. She lives in Chicago with her husband and beautiful son, and there's another on the way!

Photo Credits

Cover, pp. 1, 18, 27, 33, 36 National Park Service; p. 5 © Bettmann/Corbis; p. 7 National Archives and Records Administration; p. 8 Lake County Museum/Corbis; pp. 9, 14, 24, 31 © Raymond Gehman/Corbis; p. 10 © maps.com/Corbis; p. 11 © Corbis; pp. 16, 19, 28 © Jonathan Blair/Corbis; p. 21 Library of Congress, Prints and Photograph Division; p. 34 Jim Swindler; p. 39 Library of Congress, Geography and Map Division; p. 40 © Scott T. Smith/Corbis.

Designer: Les Kanturek; Editor: Charles Hofer;
Photo Researcher: Amy Feinberg